To my Dad and Mom,
thanks for never giving up
on me.

Get the FREE Audiobook at:
JolieCanoli.com/BonesAudio

Publishing

Copyright ©2021
by Jolie Williams and Jessica Ostrander. All rights reserved.
Published in the United States,
by Think Voyage Publishing LLC
203 Wilson Ave., West Bend, Wisconsin, 53090
Library of Congress Control Number: 2018904086
ISBN: 978-1-954695-99-3
JolieCanoli.com

BONES

created by
Jolie Canoli
& Jessica Ostrander

Jolie Canoli
And Friends

Hi!

My name is Buddy.

I am a good dog.

I have a collar.
On my collar I have a key.

My key opens a box of treasure.

I will never lose it.

I lost my key.

Dig, dig, dig.

Aha! I found...

...a bone.

...a bone.

Swim, swim, swim.

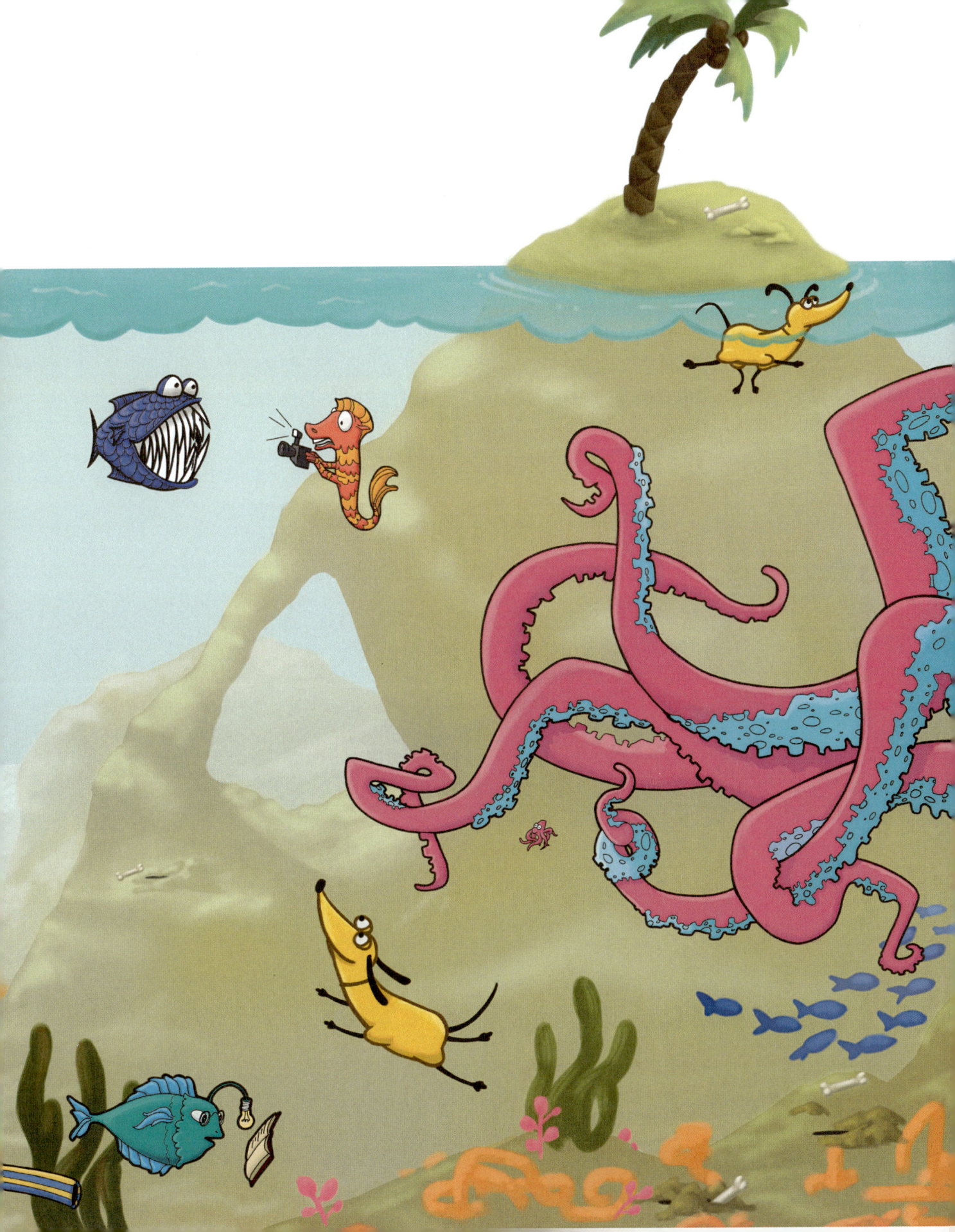

I found a bone.

...a bone.

And my key!

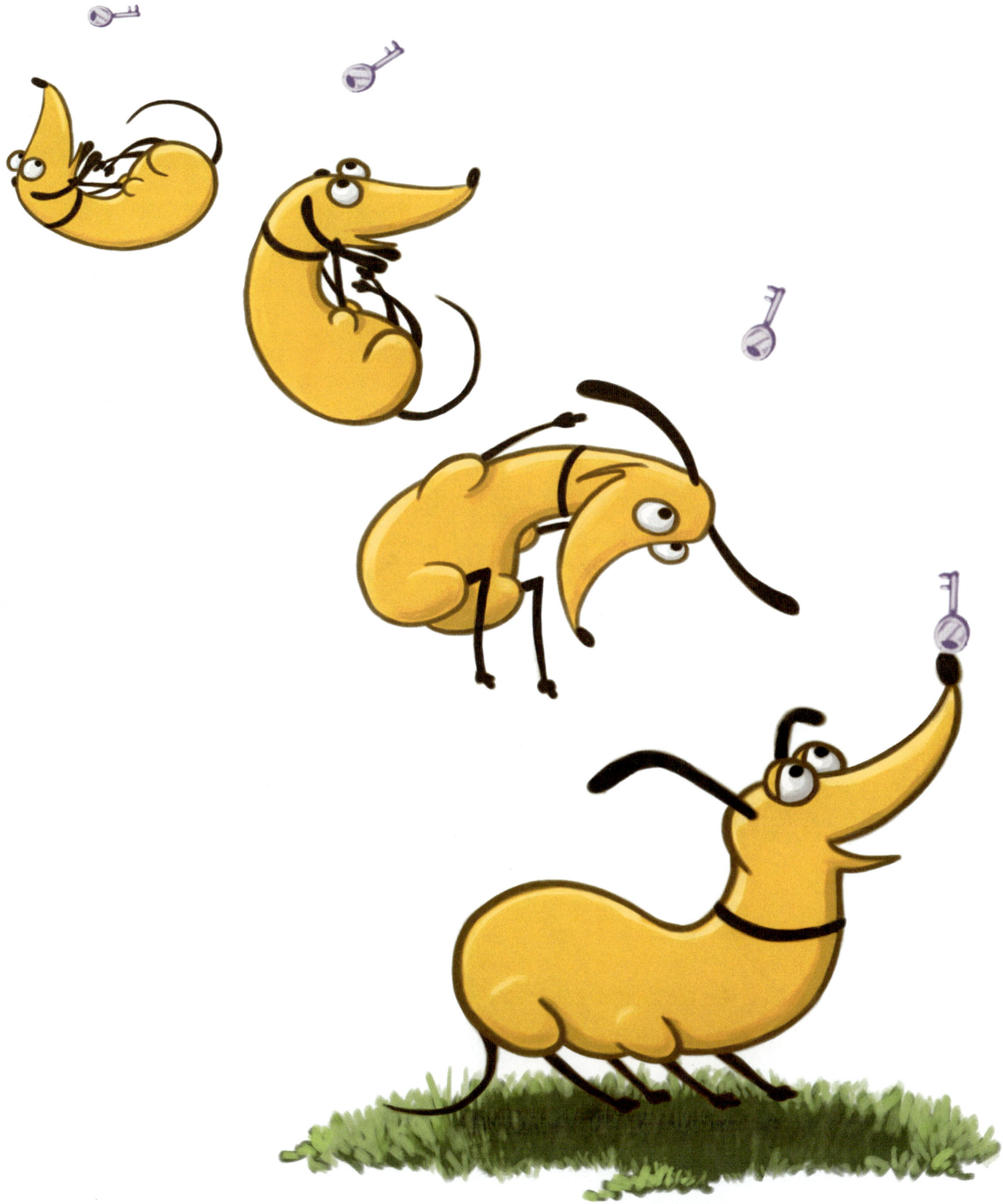

Now I will open my treasure box!

What is inside?

Bones!

Jolie Canoli (aka Dr. Jolie Williams) writes children's stories that knit humor and heart into learning. She first began writing stories for the stage. Now, as a mother of four, Jolie loves to create stories that stir children to think bigger and love better. She also illustrates, composes music, and performs internationally with her husband.

Jessica Ostrander creates oodles of doodles, bringing stories to life with vibrant creativity. She is a visual and performing artist, and art and theater educator. She believes stories make the world a better place by helping each of us discover a piece of ourselves and find where we belong.

   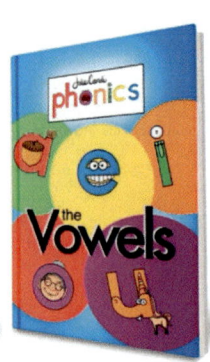 

Enjoyed this story? You'll love our others!
Find books and puppets at **JolieCanoli.com**

Bones Teachable Moments

Each time you read this book you can choose one topic below to start a meaningful conversation. Consider going the "Extra Mile" by sharing a personal story with your child.

Reading Comprehension
1. Buddy found a lot of bones. What was he actually looking for?
2. What did Buddy do once he found his key?
3. Did you guess what Buddy had in his treasure chest? Were you right?
4. Why do you think it was important to Buddy that he have the bones in the treasure chest, and not the other bones?

Precious to Me
1. Buddy's key was very precious to him. What is something that is precious to you?
2. Why is it precious to you?
3. You are so precious to me. I love you because you are… (Share 3 things that you love about your child. Here's some ideas: strong, kind, courageous, beautiful, capable, caring, creative, smart, patient, gentle, hard working, determined, energetic.)
Extra Mile- Share a fond memory of your child.

Losing Something
1. Buddy lost his key. Have you ever lost something?
2. How did you feel when you lost it?
3. Did you ever find it? How did that make you feel?
4. What did you do with your feelings?
Extra Mile- Share a time when you or your child had strong feelings and were able to use them in a good way.

Working Hard
1. Buddy worked very hard to find his lost key. Have you ever had to work very hard to do something?
2. Did you ever feel like giving up, but kept working until it was done? Were you proud that you kept working?
3. Buddy never gave up looking for his key. What is something important that you will never give up on?
Extra Mile- Let me tell you story of a time that I worked hard and never gave up.

Can you seek and find in this book:
A bush that looks like a cat, purple and green jewels, three taco fish, a sock fish, a bone flag, a sheep, and two islands shaped as bones?

Made in the USA
Las Vegas, NV
11 May 2025